# A YELLOW
# Poetry
## PAINTBOX

## CHOSEN BY JOHN FOSTER

### OXFORD
#### UNIVERSITY PRESS

Oxford University Press, Great Clarendon Street, Oxford OX2 6DP

Oxford  New York
Athens  Auckland  Bangkok  Bogotá  Buenos Aires
Calcutta  Cape Town  Chennai  Dar es Salaam
Delhi  Florence  Hong Kong  Istanbul  Karachi
Kuala Lumpur  Madrid  Melbourne  Mexico City
Mumbai  Nairobi  Paris  São Paulo  Shanghai
Singapore  Taipei  Tokyo  Toronto  Warsaw

and associated companies in
Berlin  Ibadan

© Oxford University Press 1994

Oxford is a trade mark of Oxford University Press

First published in paperback 1994
Reissued in this edition 2001

A CIP catalogue record for this book is available
from the British Library

**Illustrations by**

Renée Andriani, Jane Bottomley, Bucket, Caroline Crossland,
Paul Dowling, Fiona Dunbar, Yajia Gao, David Holmes,
Rhian Nest James, Jan Lewis, Graham Round, Jessica Thomson, Jenny Williams

ISBN 0 19 919394 0

Printed in Hong Kong

# Contents

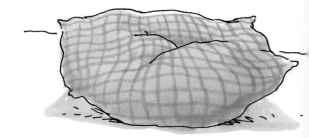

# Guess who?

Who chews a hole
  in the kitchen door?
Who makes puddles
  on the floor?

Who wags her tail
and chases the cat?
Who eats Dad's slippers
and rips up the mat?

Who tries to jump
the garden gate?
Who steals my dinner
from my plate?

Who runs to meet me
   every day?
Who rolls on her back
   when she wants to play?

Who's my best friend?
  Well, can't you guess?
My best friend is
  my puppy Jess.

*Marie Brookes*

7

# In my garden

In my garden,
My pets are free.
Sometimes they come
To play with me—
Butterflies, all kinds of bugs,
Ladybirds and snails and slugs,
Caterpillars and bumble-bees
Which live among the grass and
trees.

*Gwenda Izzet*

9

# My goldfish

My goldfish is
   the perfect pet.
She isn't any trouble.
She doesn't bark.
She doesn't mew,
   just bubbles
          bubbles
          bubbles.

My goldfish is
   the perfect pet.
She isn't any trouble.
We don't have
   to feed her much.
She doesn't need
   a rabbit hutch,
    just bubbles
       bubbles
       bubbles.

*Marie Brookes*

11

# Pet talk

Jamie has a cat,
Jimmy has a dog;
Jennie has a gerbil,
Jilly has a frog.

Mandy has a budgie,
Michael has a horse;
Maggie has a rabbit
and *I* have...

      a BABY BROTHER,
           of course!

*Judith Nicholls*

# Bonfire Night

In the night-time darkness,
In the night-time cold,
Did you spot a catherine wheel
Raining showers of gold?
Did you watch a rocket
Go zoom into the sky?
And hear a bonfire crackle
As the sparks lit up the guy?
In the night-time darkness,
In the night-time cold,
Did you clutch a sparkler
As it scattered stars of gold?

*Irene Yates*

## Christmas Eve

Nearly midnight;
still can't sleep!
Has he been yet?
Dare I peep?

Sneak out softly,
creaking floor!
Down the stairs
and through the door . . .
In the darkness
by the tree,
tightly wrapped . . .
but which for me?

Sometimes I pretend
I am an ant,
With feet so small
I tiptoe by
And no one knows
I'm there at all!

*Trevor Harvey*

# When Susie's eating custard

When Susie's eating custard,
It splashes everywhere—
Down her bib, up her nose,
All over her high chair.

She pokes it with her fingers.
She spreads it on her hair.
When Susie's eating custard,
She gets it everywhere.

*John Foster*

# When the giant comes to breakfast

When the giant comes to breakfast
He eats Corn Flakes with a spade,
Followed by a lorry load
Of toast and marmalade.
Next, he takes a dustbin
Fills it up with tea,
Drinks it all in a gulp,
And leaves the mess for me.

*John Coldwell*

*Hoo, hoo, hoo!*
Did you ever chew
a bubble-gum stew
mixed up with some custard?
*Can I have some too?*

*Judith Nicholls*

# Time for...?

Christopher Sweet tucked his feet
down to the bottom
of the warm, warm sheet.
*How many times
did the Church clock strike?
One, two, three, four, five,
six, seven, EIGHT!*

Caroline Tate is always late,
she's only just running
through the old school gate!
*How many times*
*did the school bell chime?*
*One, two, three, four, five,*
*six, seven, eight, NINE!*

Oliver Lee can't wait for tea,
school's nearly finished for him and me!
*How many rings till we're all free?*
*One, two, THREE!*

It's swallowed a sock.
We can't open the door.
It's bubbling out soap suds
All over the floor.

There's a monster that lives
In our washing machine.
It's eating our clothes,
Not washing them clean.

*John Foster*

# Princess Kirandip

At school in the week
I wear
A grey skirt and
Green jumper, just like my best friend
And we pretend we're twins.
But on Saturdays and Sundays
I wear my
Shiny, shiny blue
Kameeze and langa
With a tuni to cover my head,
All covered with silver stars—
And Tracey
Stares at me and says
'Oh, Kirandip—
You must be a princess!'

And I feel good.

*Irene Yates*

# My clean blouse

Look at my blouse!
It was clean today.
I tried very hard
To keep it that way.

Do you like my painting?
It's a bird in the sky.
But I leaned on the paper
Before it was dry.

Then at play time I joined in
A great game of chase
But I tripped on a stone
And fell flat on my face.

60

At lunch time, somebody,
Peter, I think,
Bumped into me just as I
Picked up my drink.

Then on the way home
I was splashed by a lorry.
I tried to stay clean, Mum.
Believe me. I'm sorry.

*John Coldwell*

## Index of first lines

# Acknowledgements

The Editor and Publisher are grateful for permission to include the following poems:

Marie Brookes for 'The lost sock', 'Guess who?' and 'My goldfish' all © 1991 Marie Brookes; John Coldwell for 'My clean blouse' © 1991 John Coldwell; John Foster for 'Pretending', 'Shoes', 'There's a hole in my pants' and 'When Susie's eating custard' all © 1991 John Foster; David Harmer for 'Picnic tea' © 1991 David Harmer; Trevor Harvey for 'Sometimes I pretend' © 1991 Trevor Harvey; Gwenda Izzet for 'In my garden' © 1991 Gwenda Izzet; Wendy Larmont for 'Chinese New Year' © 1991 Wendy Larmont; Judith Nicholls for 'Christmas Eve', 'Did you really?', 'Pet talk' and 'Time for . . . ?' all © 1991 Judith Nicholls; Marian Swinger for 'Eid-Mubarak' © 1991 Marian Swinger; Charles Thomson for 'Pirates' © 1991 Charles Thomson; Irene Yates for 'Adventure at breakfast time', 'Bonfire night', 'At Bimla's house last night' and 'Princess Kirandip' all © 1991 Irene Yates.